Praying the Lord's Prayer with Children

Kenneth Steven

ILLUSTRATED BY Laetitia Zink

Paulist Press
New York / Mahwah, NJ

Cover image by Laetitia Zink
Cover and book design by Lynn Else

Library of Congress Cataloging-in-Publication Data
Names: Steven, Kenneth C., 1968- author. | Zink, Laetitia, illustrator.
Title: Praying the Lord's prayer with children / by Kenneth Steven ; illustrated by Laetitia Zink.
Description: New York ; Mahwah, NJ : Paulist Press, [2023] | Audience: Ages 3–8 | Audience: Grades K–1 | Summary: "Designed for an adult to read to young children, Praying the Lord's Prayer with Children explains each phrase of this important prayer"—Provided by publisher.
Identifiers: LCCN 2022044800 (print) | LCCN 2022044801 (ebook) | ISBN 9780809168033 (hardcover) | ISBN 9780809187874 (ebook)
Subjects: LCSH: Lord's prayer—Juvenile literature.
Classification: LCC BV232 .S74 2023 (print) | LCC BV232 (ebook) | DDC 226.9/6—dc23/eng/20230123
LC record available at https://lccn.loc.gov/2022044800
LC ebook record available at https://lccn.loc.gov/2022044801

ISBN 978-0-8091-6803-3 (hardcover)
ISBN 978-0-8091-8787-4 (e-book)

Published by Paulist Press
997 Macarthur Boulevard
Mahwah, New Jersey 07430
www.paulistpress.com

Printed and bound in the
United States of America
by CG Book Printers
North Mankato, Minnesota
March 2023

Traditional

Our Father, who art in heaven, hallowed be thy name.
Thy kingdom come, thy will be done, on earth as it is in heaven.
Give us this day our daily bread, and forgive us our trespasses,
as we forgive those who trespass against us.
And lead us not into temptation
but deliver us from evil.

AMEN.

Modern English

Our Father
Who is in heaven. Your name is holy.
Your kingdom come, your will be done, on earth as it is in heaven.
Give us today our daily bread.
Forgive us our sins, as we forgive those who sin against us.
Save us from the time of trial
and deliver us from evil.

AMEN.

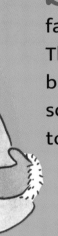

id you know the Bible says that God is your father and your mother? This might sound strange, but it's because God loves us so much that we never need to feel lonely or afraid.

Our Father

As strong and gentle
As Mommy and Daddy,
The one who cares for us,
Who never forgets us.

God is in heaven. We can't be both in heaven and on earth at the same time, but God can. We don't know exactly where heaven is, but we do know that everyone there is happy. God is love, and being close to God makes us happy.

Who art in heaven

We can't see God,
Yet God is always there,
Close enough beside us
To hear every prayer.

God's name is special—that's what "holy" and "hallowed" mean. Because of this, we honor and respect God, and we can call God our Father.

Hallowed be thy name

The one who made the mountains,
Who put the colors in the sunset,
This strong and great God
Is our own best friend.

God's kingdom is a place where people don't fight or cheat or lie. It's a place where there is real love, which is very powerful indeed. It's also a place where people are happy.

Thy kingdom come

One day, all the lying,
All the stealing and the cheating,
The sadness and the fighting
Will be gone for good.

Jesus taught us this prayer because he knew that God's will is the best thing for all of us. We need to understand that being selfish is not good for us, and that God wants the very best for each one of us.

Thy will be done, on earth as it is in heaven

We need to ask God
What God really wants for us,
Not just ask for all the things
We'd like for ourselves.

We can trust God to give us what we need, even to feed us and clothe us. When we trust God for these things, it is much easier to share what we have with anyone who needs it.

Give us this day our daily bread

Let us have enough, God,
But not want too much,
And let us have the love to share our plenty
With those who have so little.

When you owe someone something, it is called a debt. We owe God an apology if we do something wrong (this is called a sin or a trespass). We can talk to God about it—God is kind and will forgive us.

And forgive us our trespasses

Often, we do things
That make God sad,
And sometimes we forget
The things we ought to do.

God loves us so much that he forgives us willingly. And God wants us to forgive others in the same way.

As we forgive those who trespass against us

Just as God forgives us
For all that we do wrong,
So, too, we must forgive
All who are mean to us.

Sometimes life can be very difficult, so we ask God to protect us when this happens. We ask God, too, to protect us from going the wrong way and doing things that are not good for us.

And lead us not into temptation

We ask our loving God
To show us
The road that we should follow
And always be our guide.

We ask God to keep us safe from all bad things.

But deliver us from evil

We ask God to hold us
In strong hands,
And keep us every day
From all wrong ways.

Some prayer traditions add these thoughts: Everything belongs to our Creator God. We are loved so much that God cares about every hair on our heads.

For thine is the kingdom, the power, and the glory

Because God is our King
And loves us so much,
This great Creator God
Who made everything good.

Forever and ever

Be with us always,
Our friend and our guide,
Through the days of this life,
Until heaven is our home.

AMEN!

We agree! So be it!
Let us always remember
This prayer that you gave us,
To keep safe and to love.